BRITISH HISTORY

Modern Britain

1914-present

KING*f*ISHER

KINGFISHER
Kingfisher Publications Plc
New Penderel House, 283–288 High Holborn
London WC1V 7HZ
www.kingfisherpub.com

Material in this edition previously published by Kingfisher Publications Plc
in *Children's Illustrated Encyclopedia of British History* in 1992

This revised, reformatted and updated edition published by
Kingfisher Publications Plc in 2002

1TR/0202/PROSP/RNB/140MA

2 4 6 8 10 9 7 5 3 1

A CIP catalogue record for this book is available from the British Library

ISBN 0 7534 0785 X

Printed in China

Consultant: Valerie St Johnston
Editor: James Harrison,
with Jean Coppendale and Honor Head
Designer: Edward Kinsey
Proofreader: Samantha Armstrong
Indexer: Christine Bernstein
Cover design: Mike Davis

CONTENTS

MODERN BRITAIN
(1914 – PRESENT)

WORLD WAR I is often seen as a dividing line between British prosperity and decline. But this is not an accurate view because, by 1914, Britain was already losing its pre-eminence in its navy and industry, and the monarchy and House of Lords had little authority. Workers were also becoming steadily better organized, and strikes were to become frequent.

After World War II (1939-1945), Britain quickly lost her empire; the countries belonging to it were almost all independent by 1970. They remained linked in the Commonwealth of Nations.

In the modern world, it has become apparent that a small country can no longer stand alone. So Britain has become a member of other organizations: the United Nations, the North Atlantic Treaty Organization and the European Union which provide support for trade and defence.

Elizabeth II is one of the longest reigning English monarchs.

World War I

BRITAIN HAD BEEN ENJOYING a period of isolation before 1900, but the build up of the German navy and the Kaiser's ambition to acquire more colonies worried Britain. Other European rivalry over trade, colonies and military power had also been growing, and the European powers had grouped in defensive alliances. In 1902, Britain's only ally was Japan.

World War I began when a Serb student assassinated Archduke Ferdinand, heir to the Austro-Hungarian throne, in Sarajevo on June 28, 1914. When Austria declared war on Serbia, Russia, a fellow Slav nation, went to Serbia's aid. Germany supported its ally, Austria, and France was allied with Russia.

Germany had always dreaded a war on two fronts (to the east and west of its borders), so it put the Schlieffen Plan into operation. Drawn up by General von Schlieffen, the plan aimed to beat France in six weeks so that Germany could concentrate its forces against Russia.

Above: **A recruiting poster at the start of World War I with the message, "Your country needs you" from the War Minister, Lord Kitchener. Inspired by the call, volunteers crowded the recruiting offices, hoping to join up. Most people expected the war to be over by Christmas. But this soon changed when the horror of trench warfare became known.**

BRITAIN GETS DRAWN INTO WAR

The British Cabinet was divided on what steps to take. Some of its members still hoped that Britain would not have to take sides. But others feared that the Germans would take the Channel ports in France and Belgium. On August 3, 1914 the Germans invaded Belgium and started to march down towards Paris. The British then recalled their Treaty of London (1839) by which they had agreed to protect Belgian independence. It was on these grounds that Britain declared war against Germany on August 4, 1914. The BEF (British Expeditionary

Above: **Armies faced one another across a narrow strip of ground known as "No Man's Land". Behind barbed wire defences, the soldiers dug trenches in which to shelter from the gunfire. Before an attack, heavy guns fired thousands of high explosive shells at enemy lines. Then the infantry charged out of the trenches. They wore steel helmets and carried hand grenades and rifles with bayonets.**

Right: **American, British and German infantrymen during World War I. Their uniforms were cut from khaki or green cloth. French soldiers wore pale blue uniforms. The opposing sides often faced each other in trenches only a few hundred metres apart.**

German soldier

British soldier

US soldier

● **1914** Lords reject votes for women. Commons pass Irish Home Rule bill; Irish rebel in Dublin. Britain declares war on Germany. DORA (Defence of the Realm Act) passed. British troops land in France. Britain declares war on Austria-Hungary. Battle of Namur and Mons. Retreat from Mons. First battle of the Marne. Battle of the Aisne. Irish Home Rule suspended. Boers rebel. First battle of Ypres. Britain declares war on Turkey. British establish protectorate in Egypt. First Treasury notes: £1 and £10. Panama Canal opened

● **1915** HMS *Formidable* sunk. German airship bombs Britain. German blockade of Britain. Battle of Neuve Chapelle. Second battle of Ypres: Germans' first use poison gas. Allied fleets fail to force the Dardenelles. Allied troops land in Gallipoli. British liner *Lusitania* is sunk by U-boat; 124 Americans drowned. Herbert Asquith forms coalition government. Zeppelin airships over London. British take Mesopotamia. Boers surrender in South Africa. Allies withdraw from Gallipoli

● **1916** Conscription introduced. Clydeside munitions workers strike. Easter rebellion in Dublin. Battle of Jutland. HMS *Hampshire* sunk a week later: British war minister Lord Kitchener dies. National Savings begin. Daylight Saving (summer time) begins. Battle of the Somme: first tanks used. Germans shell English coast. David Lloyd George becomes PM

● **1917** British capture Baghdad. Imperial War Cabinet formed. US declares war on Germany. Battle of Arras: Canadians capture Vimy Ridge. Royal family stop using German family name: Saxe-Coburg-Gotha becomes Windsor; Battenberg becomes Mountbatten. Third battle of Ypres. Russian Revolutions: bolsheviks (communists) seize power

Force) crossed swiftly to France and helped to hold up the German advance in Belgium (at Mons) and in France (at the battle of the Marne). The Germans could not reach Paris. Both sides then took up defensive positions and within three months a line of trenches was dug from the Channel coast to the Swiss frontier. The war had reached a stalemate.

TRENCH WARFARE

The British and French troops lined up against the German troops along a front which began in the west and extended eastwards. From 1914 to 1918 the western front did not move more than 32 kilometres in any direction. In a series of horrific battles, millions of lives were lost for the gain of only a few kilometres. The trenches were built to protect the troops from machine gun fire. Soldiers ate, slept and kept guard in the trenches. However, with severe rain, the trenches became muddy, water-logged and disease-ridden. Attacks involved the troops going over the top to face the barbed wire and machine guns of the enemy. The aim was to achieve a break-through, but the machine guns pinned men down in their trenches. The area of land between the opposing forces' front-line trenches was called No Man's Land. Generals on

THE WESTERN FRONT

Farthest German advance, Sept. 1914	German Offensive, Mar.–July 1918
Front, July 1916	Front, Nov. 11th, 1918

Above: **A map showing the western front – a line of trenches which ran from the border of neutral Switzerland to the English Channel. Neither side managed to advance for more than 32 kilometres and millions lost their lives in trench warfare.**

both sides of the western front (in France and Belgium) believed in frontal attacks. The tragic result was a series of huge battles in which heavy casualties were sustained to no real purpose. Britain lost 60,000 troops on the first day of the battle of the Somme in 1916. The technical problem was that attacks on properly entrenched positions almost always failed, at the cost of many lives on both sides.

PASSCHENDAELE

One of the worst battles was the third battle of Ypres in 1917, also called Passchendaele. This battle was planned on the basis of many incorrect assessments. It was fought in torrential rain, and the troops had to wade through mud up to their waists. Conditions were made even worse by the flat, low-lying terrain of Flanders and the fact that the Allied artillery had smashed the drainage pipes. In 102 days the British advanced just eight kilometres at a cost of 400,000 lives. They captured the site of Passchendaele, a village which was completely destroyed in the fighting. The introduction of tanks promised to end the deadlock of trench warfare, but they did not arrive in sufficient numbers to make a difference in World War I.

Above: **The first tanks were used in the battle of the Somme by the British in 1916. These machines terrified the German soldiers but suffered too many mechanical failures to be fully effective.**

THE WAR AT SEA

There were only two major sea battles in World War I. The first in 1914, was when a German fleet was destroyed off the Falkland Islands. Then, in 1916, the battle of Jutland took place in which both Britain and Germany claimed victory. The German fleet never left its port of Kiel again until the end of the war, when it surrendered to the Allies. Instead, the Germans concentrated on a relatively new weapon: the submarine.

The German submarines, called U-boats, attacked all shipping, even that of neutral countries, bound for Britain and France. From 1914 to mid-1915, and later from 1917, U-boats successfully sank all ships on sight and nearly brought Britain to defeat. This led to the introduction of convoys whereby fleets of merchant ships were accompanied by a ship-of-war for protection. When American ships were sunk in 1917, the USA entered the war.

Left: **Britain needed goods and food from overseas, so it had to ensure command of the seas. But German U-boats made sailing to and from Britain dangerous for merchant and passenger ships.**

At the same time, British battleships blockaded German ports, effectively sealing them off from getting food and supplies. By the end of the war, German food stocks were very low.

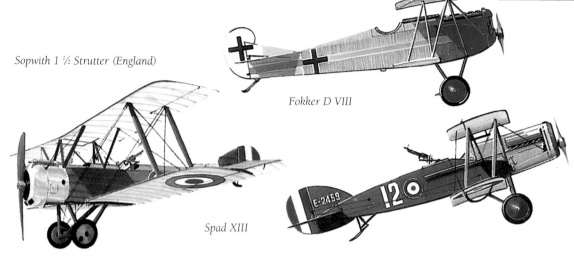

Sopwith 1 ½ Strutter (England)

Fokker D VIII

Spad XIII

THE HOME FRONT

A reforming Liberal government was in power, the last to hold office. It was headed by Herbert Asquith, who served as prime minister from 1906 to 1916. His conduct of the war drew criticism, largely that it was not dynamic enough. In 1915 a chronic shortage of shells prompted Asquith to create a Ministry of Munitions. This ministry was led by David Lloyd George.

The horrors of the Somme and the condemnation by *The Times* of Asquith's seeming inaction led to Lloyd George ousting Asquith as prime minister in December 1916.

CONSCRIPTION

Britain was the only country which did not have a huge reserve of trained men. The British Expeditionary Force contained less than 100,000 soldiers. But this professional army was wiped out in the costly battles of 1914. Volunteers flocked to join up, sometimes urged on by women who gave white feathers as a sign of cowardice to anyone of military age not in uniform. In January 1916 conscription (compulsory service) was introduced.

With so many men in the forces, women had to take over their jobs at home, gaining a big step towards the equality many of them sought. Women proved during the war that they could do "men's work".

Food was strictly rationed, largely to prevent people from hoarding supplies. National Savings were introduced to help finance the war. About 800,000 women worked in the new armaments factories to help the huge demand for weapons.

Above: **Three bi-planes from World War I. Only 12 years after the Wright brothers made their pioneering flight in North Carolina, American aircraft were being used in warfare. Although control of the air was not a deciding factor in World War I, the war led to many advances in flight technology.**

Below: **At the Versailles Peace Settlement of 1919, Germany gave back lands to France and Belgium and gave up its overseas colonies. The Habsburg monarchy ended and Poland, Czechoslovakia, Hungary and Yugoslavia became new states.**

- **1917** Balfour Declaration: Britain promises Palestine home for Jews. T.E. Lawrence joins Arab revolt. Battle of Cambrai: British capture Jerusalem. Order of the British Empire and Companions of Honour founded. Chequers estate received by British nation as residence for prime minister

- **1918** Food rationing begins (to 1919). Major German spring offensive. Second battle of the Somme halts offensive. Royal Air Force (RAF) formed, replacing Royal Flying Corps of the army. British land at Vladivostok to fight the bolsheviks. British occupy Damascus. Influenza epidemic rages. Armistice with Austria-Hungary. Armistice with Germany (November 11th) ends the war. Labour Party quits coalition. "Khaki" Election: Liberal-Conservative coalition majority 262. Women over 30 get the vote; used for the first time in December general election. House of Commons rejects proportional representation. Stonehenge presented to the nation. First oil well in Britain (Hardstoft)

EUROPE IN 1918

☐ Independent States created by war

NORWAY
FINLAND
SWEDEN
ESTONIA
LATVIA
IRISH FREE STATE
UNITED KINGDOM
DENMARK
LITHUANIA
GERMANY
U S S R
NETH.
Berlin
BELGIUM
LUX.
GERMANY
Warsaw
POLAND
Paris
FRANCE
CZECHOSLOVAKIA
SWITZ.
AUSTRIA
HUNGARY
ROMANIA
ITALY
YUGOSLAVIA
PORTUGAL
SPAIN
Corsica
Rome
BULGARIA
Madrid
Sardinia
ALBANIA
Gallipoli
GREECE
T U R K E Y
Sicily

THE EASTERN FRONT

In 1915 the Russian army faced German and Austrian troops on the eastern front, which ran from the Baltic to the Black Sea, with millions of Russian casualties. Britain and France tried to get supplies to Russia through the Dardanelles, the straits connecting the Mediterranean to the Black Sea, but the Turkish defences proved too strong. The ensuing Gallipolli campaign was also a failure for the Allies, including many ANZAC troops (from Australia and New Zealand).

THE END OF THE WAR

When a final German offensive failed in 1918, Germany's allies crumbled and German generals realized that they could not win the war. German delegates signed an armistice, and a ceasefire was ordered to take effect at 11 am on November 11, 1918, on all fronts. World War I had ended.

A DIVIDED IRELAND

When World War I broke out in August 1914, the "Irish Question" was put aside while politicians concentrated on the war. A Home Rule bill had been passed in 1914 – this would have allowed Ireland to remain as part of Great Britain, but granted it an Irish Parliament. However, the war prevented it from taking effect.

THE EASTER REBELLION

Irish frustration at Home Rule being granted and then delayed in World War I led to the Easter Rebellion on Good Friday 1916. The Fenian Irish Republican Brotherhood seized Dublin's public buildings. After four days of fighting, they surrendered. All but one of 15 leaders were executed. Eamon de Valera, the survivor, was spared execution only because he had been born in America. This harsh treatment made them heroes and gave support to a movement called *Sinn Fein* (Ourselves Alone). In the general election of 1918, the Sinn Fein Party won 73 seats at Westminster which it refused to take up. In an Act of 1920 Ireland was divided, with Parliaments at Belfast and Dublin. The IRA (Irish Republican Army), which demanded a united republican Ireland, started a war against this Act, killing government officials and policemen. The Black and Tans, British troops, sent to reinforce the RIC (Royal Irish Constabulary), led to more violence.

Below: **The Easter Rising of 1916 brought fierce fighting in Dublin. Civil war followed in 1922-1923 and an early victim of the conflict was Michael Collins. He was shot by republicans in 1922 for signing the treaty which created the Irish Free State but excluded the six northern counties.**

● **1919** War with Afghanistan. German East Africa handed over to Britain: renamed Tanganyika. German fleet scuttled at Scapa Flow. Lady Astor becomes first woman MP. First Atlantic aeroplane crossing by J.W. Alcock and A.W. Brown. First flight to Australia (Ross Smith), in 135 hours. League of Nations formed. Indian massacre at Amritsar. Lloyd George attends the Paris Peace Conference. British troops help anti-communists in Russian Civil War

● **1920** Former East African Protectorate becomes Kenya colony. Riots in Belfast against Irish independence. Admission of women degree students to Oxford for first time. Church of Wales disestablished. Unknown Soldier buried in Westminster Abbey. Palestine comes under British control

● **1921** Unemployment payments increased. British Legion founded. Irish Free State set up

● **1922** Fascists take power in Italy. Michael Collins murdered. Lloyd George coalition falls: Bonar Law (Conservative) becomes PM. British Broadcasting Company is founded. Geddes Axe cuts public spending. Gandhi imprisoned. IRA shoot British Field Marshal. Tutankhamen's tomb discovered

Right: **The traditional flag of Ireland was a blue flag with a golden harp.**

Left: **Today's Irish flag dates from 1919. Orange was adopted by the Protestants after William of Orange and the white stands for peace.**

Right: **The former flag of Northern Ireland, which today is only used as a loyalist emblem. The red upraised hand is an ancient symbol of Ulster.**

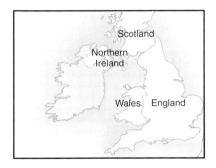

Left: **Great Britain is comprised of England, Scotland and Wales. With Northern Ireland, it becomes the United Kingdom.**

who agreed with the treaty like Collins, and those, including Eamon de Valera, who still wanted full independence for a united Ireland. The links between the Irish Free State and the United Kingdom were gradually broken during the 1930s. Following the abdication of Edward VIII, Ireland removed mention of the Crown from its constitution. In 1937 Ireland ended the Free State and proclaimed itself the Independent Republic of Ireland, or Eire. Many Roman Catholics in Northern Ireland refused to accept the division and relations between Catholics and Protestants became strained.

THE GENERAL STRIKE

The effects of World War I caused a huge strain on many nations' economies and employers wanted to cut wages. The General Strike of 1926 was called by most of Britain's major trade unions in support of miners who were fighting threatened wage cuts, but it failed because the government was able to organize volunteers to run essential services such public transport. The strike lasted nine days.

Below: **Crowds cheer as a bus is stopped during the General Strike of 1926. The original dispute was between miners and mine owners who wanted to cut wages by 25 percent. The owners shut the mines and other public workers – in steel, newspapers, electricity, transport and gas – all went on strike. Troops and volunteers with government support worked successfully to keep services running.**

ULSTER AND THE UNIONISTS

Six of the nine northern provinces of the country – together called Ulster – were determined to remain in union with England. The six were mainly Protestant, and wanted no part in an all-Irish, chiefly Catholic, Parliament. Despite having already agreed in principle to Home Rule for all Ireland, the English government gave in to unionist pressure. Lloyd George's treaty of 1921 gave the 26 southern counties of Ireland – called the Irish Free State – independence. It was signed with the Sinn Fein leaders, including Michael Collins who had led the IRA against the RIC. It was an attempt to end the violence and bloodshed, but the six northern counties were excluded from independence by their own wish to remain in the Union with Britain, and this led to a civil war in 1922-1923 between those

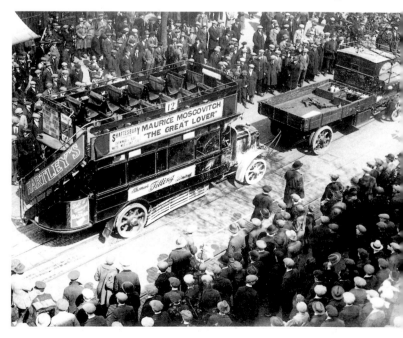

Left: In October 1935, 200 unemployed men marched to London from Jarrow in northeast England. They were protesting about unemployment which had reached about 68 percent of the workers in their area. The closure of the shipbuilding yard on the River Tyne had sparked the march. The men carried a petition and gathered much support and attention to unemployment along the way. But despite a lot of publicity the government virtually ignored their protest and the men went home again. Nevertheless, their march became a landmark of the Great Depression.

THE GREAT DEPRESSION

The world economic crisis known as the Great Depression started in the United States in 1929. Factories had been producing more goods than people could afford; workers had to work part-time and the reduced wages from reduced hours meant people could afford still less.

When the American stockmarket on Wall Street crashed in October 1929, it caused a collapse in world trade. When the United States and other countries stopped buying goods, British exporters saw their markets disappear.

Unemployment rose sharply, reaching almost three million by 1931. The worst unemployment was in the old industrial areas such as South Wales, Lancashire, Yorkshire and Clydeside. Unemployed workers queued up once a week to get their unemployment benefit (known as the dole) – money that was barely enough to live on. The government could not afford the high cost of the dole and faced a financial crisis. The economy recovered only slowly through the 1930s. As traditional industries of coal, iron and steel, textiles and shipbuilding declined, new industries such as manufacturing motorcars and electrical goods began to expand.

LEISURE

The 1930s saw an increase in leisure activities. People enjoyed a Sunday afternoon drive to the country in the new cheaper Morris, Austin and Ford cars. However, only about one family in ten owned a car, so motorbikes with side-cars and buses taking people on day trips and seaside holidays became popular. Visits to the cinema, to see the "Talkies" that had replaced silent films, became very popular. Odeon cinemas in the huge American style with restaurants and dance floors could be found in most large urban centres.

Below: The 1930 Matchless Silver Hawk. Motorbikes were popular with people who could not afford a car.

Left: Many young wealthy women in the 1920s scandalized their elders with their sophisticated evening clothes and their fast lifestyle. Many enjoyed jazz music and dancing.

HOUSING IN THE 1930s

There was a boom in the building of private houses, with some three million built in this decade. Many of these were built in so-called ribbon developments along roads into towns. People became interested in labour-saving devices, home comforts and entertainments such as gramophones, the wireless (radio), vacuum cleaners and refrigerators.

IMPERIAL TALKS

Imperial Conferences, the forerunners of today's Commonwealth Conferences, were held in 1926 and 1930. As a result of their discussions, the British Parliament passed the Statute of Westminster in 1931, which defined the laws concerning the independence of the dominions and their allegiance to the British monarchy more clearly.

The dominions were Canada, Australia, New Zealand, South Africa, the Irish Free State and Newfoundland. Allegiance to the Crown was, as now, the unifying factor. The statute also laid down that changes to royal titles and the succession to the throne had to be decided by the parliaments of all the dominions as well as that of the United Kingdom.

● **1923** Britain criticizes French and Belgian occupation of the Rhur. Benito Mussolini challenges the League of Nations over Corfu. Stanley Baldwin becomes PM (Conservative). General election produces hung Parliament

● **1924** First Labour government: Ramsay MacDonald PM. General election after only eight months returns Conservatives. British Empire exhibition opens. Britain's first national airline, Imperial Airways, is set up. Leigh Mallory and Irvine die below peak of Everest. Eric Liddell and Harold Abrahams win gold medals in Olympics. Indian campaigner for Indian independence Mahatma Gandhi goes on hunger strike in his efforts to persuade Britain to grant Home Rule. Winston Churchill becomes Chancellor of the Exchequer

● **1925** Cyprus becomes Crown colony. Unemployment Insurance Act passed. Britain builds Singapore naval base. First white lines on roads and first traffic lights introduced

● **1926** General Strike in Britain. Reading University founded. J.L. Baird demonstrates how television works. *Winnie the Pooh* is published

● **1927** IRA kill Kevin O'Higgins, Irish Minister of Justice. Trades Disputes Act: certain strikes and lockouts are declared illegal

● **1928** Women get the vote at 21. Alexander Fleming discovers penicillin mould in his laboratory. J.L. Baird demonstrates colour television

Right: In 1928 the British bacteriologist Alexander Fleming discovered the mould from which he developed the drug penicillin. This cured previously fatal diseases.

Left: Scottish engineer John Logie Baird (1888-1946) was the first to transmit a television picture by radio waves in 1926. His invention led to the first television sets and broadcasting companies.

EDWARD AND MRS SIMPSON

When George V died in 1936, his eldest son, Edward VIII, was 41 and unmarried. As Prince of Wales he had acquired great personal popularity, both at home and in the empire. Edward was aware of the social problems of the time, and had made public remarks about both slums and unemployment which earned widespread approval. However, the government saw this as political meddling and Edward spent much of his time living in France with his closest friend, Mrs Wallis Simpson. She was an American with one divorced husband and another whom she was divorcing.

Edward's infatuation with Mrs Simpson was the talk of the world's press, but by a voluntary agreement the British newspapers avoided all mention of it. The prime minister, Stanley Baldwin, spoke to the King about Mrs Simpson. Edward declared that he wanted to marry her, and proposed a morganatic marriage, a marriage in which Mrs Simpson would be his wife but not his queen. Baldwin consulted the dominions. They were against the King's proposal, and so were most of the people in Britain. Edward chose to abdicate (give up the throne) in 1936 and married Mrs Simpson in 1937.

Above: **Amy Johnson (1903-1941) an English pilot, was the first woman to fly solo, in 1930, from England to Australia.**

Below: **The Duke and Duchess of Windsor, formerly King Edward VIII and Mrs Wallis Simpson. After their marriage in 1937 they lived mainly in France.**

- **1931** National Government formed under Ramsay MacDonald; 3 million unemployed and dole cut by 10 percent. Whipsnade Zoo opened. First London trolley bus. Statute of Westminster drawn up

- **1932** Eamon de Valera elected President of Ireland. Former Labour MP Oswald Mosley starts British Union of Fascists. James Chadwick discovers neutrons. Jobless organize hunger marches

- **1933** Nazis take power in Germany. Gandhi released after hunger strike in jail. Oxford Union votes "not to fight for king and country". ICI company invents polythene

- **1934** Driving tests introduced. Liner *Queen Mary* launched with aid from government to help unemployment. First Mersey Tunnel opened. Manchester Central Library opens. Composer Edward Elgar dies

- **1935** Anti-Catholic riots in Belfast. Green Belt around London established to protect countryside from urban expansion. Robert Watson-Watt builds first practicable radar. Paperback revolution: Allen Lane founds Penguin Books. 48 km/h speed limit and crossing beacons introduced. Ramsay MacDonald retires: Stanley Baldwin (Conservative) heads National Government. Anglo-German Naval Pact allows German naval expansion. Lawrence of Arabia dies in motor bike accident. Clement Attlee becomes new Labour leader. Unemployed shipyard workers march from Jarrow to London

- **1936** George V dies: succeeded by son, Edward VIII. BBC starts regular TV service. Edward VIII abdicates: succeeded by brother, George VI (to 1952). British volunteers fight in Spanish Civil War. Hitler's remilitarization of the Rhineland goes unopposed. Pinewood film studios open. *Queen Mary* makes maiden voyage. Crystal Palace in destroyed in fire

GEORGE VI

Edward's successor was his brother Albert, Duke of York, who took the title of George VI in 1936. The new king was a quiet, shy man with a speech impediment. But he had the great advantage of a beautiful and popular wife, Elizabeth (later known as the Queen Mother), and together they gained the respect and affection of the people.

George VI had an extremely difficult reign, during which he took upon himself the task of maintaining the morale of the British people throughout World War II.

THE THREAT OF HITLER'S GERMANY

Like the new prime minister Neville Chamberlain, George VI had hoped that a peaceful solution could be found to Europe's growing insecurity. This was caused by German naval expansion and rebuilding its military might under Adolf Hitler who had become the Fuhrer, or leader, of the country in 1934. He wanted to avenge the humiliation brought to Germany by the Versailles Peace Settlement of 1919. Chamberlain pursued a policy of appeasement; that is, he sought to make concessions to Hitler in the hope that peace would be maintained.

Once it was evident that Hitler was set on the military domination of Europe, George VI did everything he could to encourage the countries which owed allegiance to him to play their part in the war. He took an active part in the war himself, and with his wife inspected the bomb damage of the Blitz and visited munitions factories. Through his efforts the royal family became an emotional rallying point in the struggle against Nazi Germany.

Above: **George VI (1936-1952) the second son of George V, had not expected to be king. However, Edward VIII's sudden abdication meant that George VI became king without any chance to prepare for the role. George and his queen, Elizabeth, became a focus for all classes struggling through the turbulent years of World War II. Their devotion to duty in the war helped them to re-establish the reputation of the monarchy after the problems caused by the abdication crisis.**

Right: On September 27, 1938 Queen Elizabeth launched the Cunard-White Star liner named for her, the *Queen Elizabeth*. It was the largest ship of its day.

- **1937** Air raid precautions planned. Irish Free State becomes Eire. Frank Whittle builds first jet engine. Stanley Baldwin retires: Neville Chamberlain becomes PM

- **1938** National register for war service. Women's Voluntary Service founded. *Queen Elizabeth* (largest-ever liner) is launched. Britain allows Hitler's *Anschluss*, which is a union with Austria. Terrorist bombings in Palestine. *Mallard* sets locomotive speed record. Neville Chamberlain meets Adolf Hitler in attempt to resolve Sudeten crisis in which Hitler sought to reclaim the Sudetenland area of Czechoslovakia, which Germany was forced to give back after World War I. The Munich Agreement is signed, the height of appeasement, and Sudetenland is given to Germany. This fails to satisfy Hitler and German troops take over the whole of Czechoslovakia in March. Again many protests are made but no action is taken

- **1939** Morden-Finchley tube line constructed. Britain and France promise to support Poland, Greece and Romania against German aggression. Conscription introduced. George VI visits Canada and US. John Cobb sets land speed record of 594 km/h. Russo-German pact. First British transatlantic airmail service begins. Germans invade Poland. Britain and France declare war. Leaflet raids on Germany: the Phoney War period. Battle of the River Plate

- **1940** Food rationing starts. Women get old age pension at 60. Germans invade Norway and Denmark. Neville Chamberlain resigns: Winston Churchill forms coalition. Germans invade Netherlands, Belgium and France. Home Guard formed. Fire-watching compulsory. British forces evacuated from Dunkirk in northern France. Penicillin developed as antibiotic. French surrender. Battle of Britain. The Blitz: London the main target. The George Cross instituted

World War II

BRITAIN HAD APPEASED GERMANY when the Nazi government of Adolf Hitler marched into Austria and then into Czechoslovakia. But Hitler's attack on Poland, a country which Britain had pledged to help, brought Britain and France into the war. On September 3, 1939 they declared war on Germany.

Britain's lack of military readiness meant that nothing could be done to help Poland. For the first seven months there was a "Phoney War", in which little happened that affected Britain directly, apart from a blackout against air-raids, food rationing and the evacuation of children from city areas to the relative safety of the country.

WINSTON CHURCHILL

The sudden unleashing of Hitler's war machine on Denmark and Norway led to a crisis of confidence in the government of Neville Chamberlain. An all-party coalition was called for, and by general consent the choice of leader fell on Winston Churchill. He had been in the political wilderness since 1929. Throughout the 1930s his had been a lone voice warning of the possibility of war and the need to prepare. Churchill had a lot of energy and a fertile mind, which gave him the qualities needed by a wartime leader.

THE BATTLE OF THE ATLANTIC

The battle which nearly defeated Britain was the battle of the Atlantic – a naval battle which lasted from 1941 throughout the war. German U-boats (submarines) sank hundreds of Allied ships that were bringing vital food and supplies to Britain. The use of convoys, and help from the United States even before it entered the war, gradually reduced the losses. The British navy managed to destroy three powerful German battleships: the *Graf Spey*, *Bismark*, and *Tirpitz*.

Above: **Sir Winston Churchill (1874-1965) was a soldier, writer and statesman who led Britain through World War II. He became prime minister in May 1940.**

Below: **Adolf Hitler (1889-1945) was dictator of Germany from 1933 to 1945. He created the Nazi party, and his aggressive policies led to the outbreak of World War II.**

● **1941** Double Summer Time introduced. House of Commons bombed. Lend-Lease: US aid for Britain. Winston Churchill and US President Franklin Delano Roosevelt sign Atlantic Charter. Clothes rationing begins (to 1949). Conscription for women introduced. Russia invaded by Germany, and becomes an Ally. HMS *Ark Royal* is sunk. Japanese attack American naval base at Pearl Harbor, Hawaii: US brought into the war. British Eighth Army advances and retreats in Egypt and Libya

● **1942** Term United Nations first used. Japanese take Malaya, Singapore, Burma and Hong Kong. Baedeker raids: Germans bomb Bath and other cultural centres in Britain. British invade Madagascar. Mediterranean island of Malta resists continual attack: awarded the George Cross. India to get dominion status. Oxfam founded. Commando raid on Dieppe, France. Battle of El Alamein, Egypt: Allies begin final advance across Libya. Allies land in western north Africa. Economist Sir William Beveridge produces plan for social security

● **1943** Winston Churchill and President Roosevelt meet at Casablanca, Morocco. North Africa cleared of Germans and Italians. Allies land in Sicily. Allies invade mainland Italy. Italy surrenders, joins the Allies. Churchill, Roosevelt and Joseph Stalin of Russia meet at Teheran, Persia (now Iran)

THE WAR IN AFRICA

Italy, Germany's ally, joined the war in 1940, and tried to capture Egypt and the Suez Canal from its colony in Libya. The fighting raged to and fro in the Western Desert, until by July 1942 a combined Italian and German force had advanced to within 100 kilometres of Alexandria.

Three months later the British and Commonwealth armies, under new commanders (Generals Alexander and Montgomery), broke the German/Italian forces in the battle of El Alamein. By May 1943 North Africa was clear of the enemy, and two months later the Allies landed in Sicily. By October Italy had surrendered and changed sides to support the Allies.

P-51 Mustang

Spitfire

Messerschmitt

THE D-DAY INVASION OF EUROPE

The invasion of Europe by Allied forces took 18 months to prepare. D-Day, the first assault, came on June 6, 1944, when an Allied force stormed ashore on the Normandy coast. A force of 3,000,000 men had assembled in Britain; and 11,000 aircraft, 5,000 large ships and 4,000 smaller landing craft took them across the Channel. The first wave of infantry and armoured troops waded ashore at 6.30 am under a cloudy sky. It was helped by Allied air superiority.

Above: **Hitler planned to invade Britain. He began with a series of daylight air-raids to cripple the coastal defences.**
In the desperate battle of Britain, German bombers and Messerschmitts were fought off by RAF (Royal Air Force) Spitfires. Foiled, Hitler cancelled his invasion plans. The Germans then switched to a series of intensive night-bombing raids, first on London and then on other industrial centres like Coventry. This became known as "the Blitz" – short for *Blitzkrieg* (the German word for lightning war). Air-raid sirens became a well-known sound. The Blitz eased in May 1941, when the Nazi bombers were switched to attack Russian targets.

Right: **Allied troops land on a Normandy beach on D-Day, June 6, 1944, to start the liberation of France. It was the greatest sea invasion in history.**

THE WAR IN THE EAST

The Japanese attack on Pearl Harbor, an American naval base in Hawaii, in December 1941 brought the US into the war against Japan and its ally, Germany. By May 1942 the Japanese had overrun British territories in the Far East and then threatened Australia and India. Much of the Allied counter-attack in the Far East was carried out by American and Australian forces. The British fought in Burma to protect India, aided by a commando force, the Chindits.

THE END OF THE WAR

The war in Europe dragged on until the beginning of May 1945. Then, with his armies retreating, and constant bombing knocking out his oil supplies and industries, Hitler committed suicide, and the Germans surrendered. Britain celebrated May 8th as VE-day (Victory in Europe).

The war with Japan threatened to be a much longer affair. But in August the Allies launched a new and terrifying weapon. They dropped two atomic bombs on Japan, and within days the Japanese surrendered. British and American scientists had been working on the bomb for several years, in the greatest secrecy. VJ-day was celebrated on September 2. Events to mark the 50th anniversary of both VE and VJ day took part across the country in 1995, amid much celebration and remembrance.

Valentine

Tiger 1E

M-26 Pershing

Left: The British *Valentine* tank first saw action in the Western Desert. Germany's *Tiger* tank was one of the most powerful with armour 10 cm thick. The American *Pershing* tank had a speed of 50 km/h.

Right: The first atomic bombs were dropped by the United States in World War II, on the Japanese cities of Hiroshima and Nagasaki. The destruction the bombs caused was horrific, 200,000 people were killed and about as many people, over a wide area, were injured.

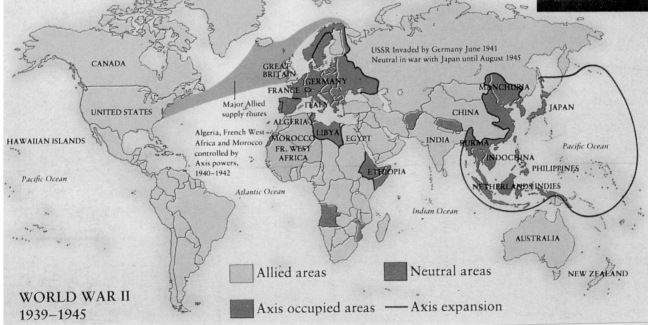

Left: By 1941 Germany had conquered most of Europe and entered North Africa. By 1942 the Japanese had overrun most of Southeast Asia and threatened Australia. Italy, Germany and Japan formed the Axis Powers; Britain, France, the US and Russia the Allied Powers.

CANADA

GREAT BRITAIN

USSR Invaded by Germany June 1941
Neutral in war with Japan until August 1945

FRANCE
GERMANY
ITALY

MANCHURIA

UNITED STATES

Major Allied supply routes

ALGERIA

CHINA

JAPAN

HAWAIIAN ISLANDS

Algeria, French West Africa and Morocco controlled by Axis powers, 1940–1942

MOROCCO
FR. WEST
AFRICA

LIBYA
EGYPT

INDIA

BURMA

Pacific Ocean

Pacific Ocean

ETHIOPIA

INDOCHINA

PHILIPPINES

Atlantic Ocean

NETHERLANDS INDIES

Indian Ocean

AUSTRALIA

NEW ZEALAND

WORLD WAR II
1939–1945

Allied areas

Axis occupied areas

Neutral areas

Axis expansion

Left: Excited crowds outside Buckingham Palace wait for the royal family to appear on VE (Victory in Europe) day, May 8, 1945. The royal family played a vital role during the war, helping to maintain morale. The king and queen refused to be evacuated from London and would frequently visit bombed areas to offer their support.

- **1944** Pay-As-You-Earn tax scheme introduced. New air-raids on London. National Health Service proposed. D-Day: Allied armies invade Normandy. Flying-bomb (V1) raids on London begin. Education Act plans to raise school-leaving age. Blackout restrictions lifted. Antwerp and Brussels liberated. British land on French Riviera. Battle of the Bulge (last major German offensive). First V2 rocket bombs launched. British paratroop attack on Arnhem (Netherlands) fails

- **1945** British 14th Army opens offensive in Burma. Churchill, Roosevelt and Stalin confer at Yalta, Crimea. Germans surrender (May 7). Coalition breaks up: Churchill forms Conservative caretaker government. General election: Labour landslide (Labour 393, Conservatives 213, Liberals 12, others 22): Clement Attlee PM. Allies meet at Potsdam June-July. Atomic bombs dropped on Hiroshima and Nagasaki, Japan surrenders: World War II ends

FOCUS ON THE WAR EFFORT

World War II had a huge impact on the lives of ordinary people. Everyone expected extensive bombing raids on British cities. So in the summer of 1939 over 1,500,000 children were evacuated to stay with families in the countryside. In London and Liverpool, many people who remained had to sleep on the underground station platforms during air-raids. Others sought refuge in Anderson shelters in their gardens. Blackout curtains kept all lights hidden, and wardens went round to ensure this. As food was rationed, people were encouraged to "Dig for Victory" and grew their own food in allotments and back gardens and on any available piece of land.

PLANNING FOR A WELFARE STATE

Even when the war was at its height the government began planning for peace. In 1942 the economist Sir William Beveridge brought out a government report on Social Insurance and Allied Services, which laid the foundations for the modern welfare state. Beveridge proposed that free unemployment benefit, health treatment, sickness pay, retirement pensions and family allowances should all be combined in one simple scheme.

In 1944 the Minister of Education, R.A. Butler (known as Rab Butler), sponsored the Butler Act which provided for three stages of free education (primary, secondary and further) and introduced the grammar school and secondary modern school systems. It also planned that the school-leaving age should be raised from 14 to 16.

LABOUR SWEEPS TO POWER

The coalition government which had fought the war did not survive long after the end of fighting in Europe. There had been no election for nearly ten years – twice the normal time allowed and people wanted a change. So Churchill resigned, and a general election was held in 1945.

The result was a sweeping victory for the Labour Party, which was returned with a majority of 146. Its leader, Clement Attlee, who had been deputy to Churchill in the coalition government, became prime minister. Labour won with a policy of social and economic reconstruction which was similar to the Beveridge plan, while the Conservatives bore the blame for much of the hardship and discontent of the 1930s.

Below: Many women joined the armed forces or took up the call to "dig for victory" by joining the Women's Land Army.

AMERICAN AID

Labour's plans for the future were greatly hampered by thehuge debts left by the war. Britain's exports had dropped sharply, while it had to borrow hugely to pay for supplies. It had also had to sell off a quarter of its overseas investments thereby losing the income from them. Worse still, the Lend-Lease scheme, by which the United States provided goods on a more or less free-gift basis, abruptly ended. Britain had also lost millions of tonnes of merchant shipping. A huge loan from the United States, called the Marshall Loan, went only part way towards bridging the financial gap. For several years after the war had ended people in Britain faced clothes and food rationing.

NATIONAL INSURANCE

Despite financial difficulties, the Labour government managed to carry through part of its welfare programme including the introduction of National Insurance against old age and unemployment: every man and woman who worked had to pay some money every week into a national insurance fund – as did the employers. Then, if they became unable to work through illness, having a baby, unemployment or retirement, they could claim financial benefits (support). The National Health Service was launched in 1948, providing free health care. Even funerals were paid for, so for the first time the government helped its citizens "from cradle to grave" as William Beveridge proposed. Legal aid was also established to help poor people meet the cost of court cases.

NATIONALIZATION

The Labour government also believed that the major utilities of the country, such as coal, electricity and the railways, should not be owned by private companies run for shareholders' profits but should be owned and run by the government in the interests of the British public.

With this in mind, the coal mines were nationalized in 1947, the railways, electricity and gas in 1948, and the steel industry and the Bank of England. The government hoped that the profits made from these industries could be spent on the new machinery and equipment needed to run them properly.

CHANGES IN THE HOUSE OF LORDS

The Labour government reduced the power of the House of Lords to delay bills that the Commons had passed. In 1911 this power had been set at two years; a new act in 1949 reduced it to one. Another reform removed the right of businessmen to have a vote for their business premises as well as at home. One person, one vote became the rule. The House of Lords continued to be criticized because all its members, apart from the bishops and the Law Lords, inherited their titles and their right to sit in the Lords.

Below: **In August 1948 the Olympic Games were held in London. These were the first games to be held for twelve years.**

● **1945** Lend-lease ends: financial crisis. United Nations inaugurated. US lends Britain $3.75 billion. Family allowances begin. Labour government elected; Clement Attlee PM. German war trials begin in Nuremberg. George Orwell's *Animal Farm* published

● **1946** Trade Disputes Act (1927) repealed. Bank of England nationalized. New Towns Act passed. Civil Aviation nationalized. Churchill's Iron Curtain speech at Fulton, Missouri. BBC resumes TV (suspended since 1939), with 12,000 viewers. Bread rationed (world shortage). BBC Third Programme begins (forerunner of Radio 3). National Health Act

● **1947** Coal mines nationalized. Fuel crisis: shortage of coal. Road transport nationalized. India partitioned to form independent India and Pakistan. First atomic pile installed at Harwell. Princess Elizabeth marries Philip Mountbatten, Duke of Edinburgh. School-leaving age raised to 15

● **1948** Railways, power and gas industries are nationalized. British control in Palestine comes to an end. Act declares that all Commonwealth citizens are automatically British. Bread rationing ends. Corporal punishment is abolished. National Health Service is established. Olympic Games are held in London. Nottingham University is founded

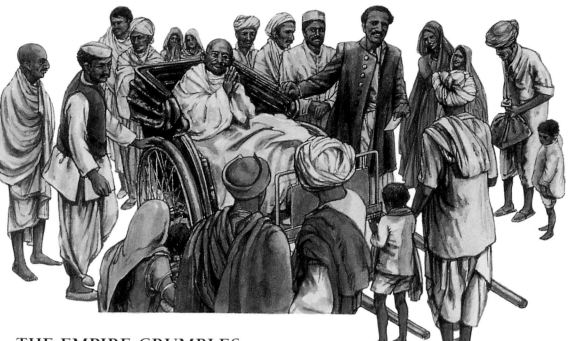

Left: **Mahatma Gandhi led India to independence from the British in 1947. He did this by organizing passive (non-violent) resistance to British rule on a mass scale and was imprisoned several times. Gandhi was assassinated in 1948 by a Hindu fanatic.**

THE EMPIRE CRUMBLES

After World War II a wave of nationalism in Britain's colonies was accompanied by a growing belief among the British that having an empire was morally unjustified and uneconomic. As a result, the dominions (former British empire colonies) were swiftly given independence. In 1947 the Indian empire was split into two countries, India and Pakistan. This led to mass emigration and hideous massacres across India as it did not go far enough towards solving religious conflicts. Burma (now Myanmar) and Ceylon (now Sri Lanka) both became independent in 1948. Burma opted to leave the Commonwealth, as did Ireland, which declared itself an independent republic in 1949.

CHANGE OF GOVERNMENT

After five difficult years the Labour Party went into the general election of 1950 considerably divided, and although it won, its overall majority was cut to only six. After struggling on for 20 months, it called another election with a manifesto which made little mention of any further nationalization – once the main plank of the Labour platform.

The Conservatives were returned with a majority of 16. Winston Churchill, now 76, became prime minister again. Hardly had the dust of the election settled than George VI, who had survived an operation for lung cancer, died suddenly in his sleep. He was succeeded by his 25-year-old daughter, Elizabeth II, who had been prepared for her future role as queen since childhood.

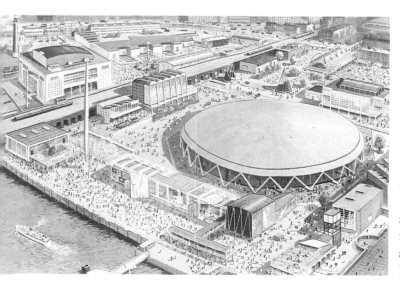

Left: **The Festival of Britain took place in 1951 on London's South Bank. It was a centenary celebration of the Great Exhibition of 1851 and also promoted British-made products, design and architecture. The Festival Hall and Dome of** Discovery can be seen here. British people, homes and gardens, schools, sport, television and cinema were all celebrated, and household names like Ovaltine, Creda, Heinz, Hoover, Morris, EMI and Lloyds Bank were featured.

THE COLD WAR

Despite having been joined by Russia as an ally during World War II, Britain and the United States became increasingly worried about Russia's plans in Eastern Europe (and the world) after the war. British intelligence services were convinced that Russia wanted to dominate the world with its Communist system.

Under the Soviet leader, Joseph Stalin, Russian military might was formidable, but the West had atomic weapons to counter this. However, when Russia developed its own atomic bomb in 1949, and a more powerful hydrogen bomb in 1953, worsening east-west relations reached a stalemate: a Cold War developed, based on fear and calculations about who could defeat whom in a nuclear war. This stalemate dominated foreign policy until Mikhail Gorbachev announced cuts in Soviet forces in central Europe in 1988 and Soviet Communism collapsed.

THE KOREAN WAR

The fear of the spread of Communism also brought Britain into the Korean War of 1950-1953, often called the Forgotten War. Communist North Korea, backed by China, invaded South Korea across the 38th Parallel – a Cold War dividing line drawn up by the increasingly hostile allies after World War II. The West suspected that Stalin had a hand in stirring up and supporting this conflict, and sent troops in to support South Korea.
Some 750 British troops lost their lives in this three-year war.

The Korean War put a great strain on Britain's economy, at a time when it needed to keep pace with Germany and other countries in the post-war recovery period.

THE SUEZ CRISIS

After World War II Britain retained a garrison in Egypt to guard the Suez Canal – a vital link between Britain and the Far East. But Egypt's new ruler, Colonel Nasser, demanded that the British withdraw, and in June 1956 the last troops left the Canal Zone.

Meanwhile Nasser was trying to obtain a loan from Britain and other countries to finance the Aswan High Dam across the River Nile. Anti-British broadcasts on the radio by Egypt, plus doubts about the country's ability to repay any loans, led to the withdrawal of all offers of help. At this Nasser nationalized the Canal, a move which threatened access for other countries.

The newly-formed state of Israel, always at loggerheads with its Arab neighbours, proposed a plan whereby Israel would attack Egypt, giving Britain and France, the chief shareholders in the Suez Canal, an excuse to intervene and restore order. This plan was welcomed by the prime minister, Anthony Eden, who had succeeded Churchill in 1955. Eden had been a skilful foreign secretary, but his skill now deserted him.

Israel attacked Egypt as planned: Britain and France demanded a withdrawal of troops on both sides, and proposed an Anglo-French garrison for the Canal. Egypt refused and this was a signal for Anglo-French troops to invade. Pressure from the United Nations, led by the United States, and from Russia forced an immediate withdrawal of the British and French forces. A few months later Anthony Eden resigned as prime minister, due to ill health, and retired from political life.

Left: **On May 29, 1953, Sir Edmund Hillary of New Zealand and Tenzig Norgay, a Nepalese Sherpa tribesman, ascended the summit of Everest. They became the first to scale** the highest mountain in the world, just as Elizabeth II ascended to the throne. These two newsworthy events were reported at the same time on the BBC World Service.

Elizabeth II

IN 1,000 YEARS OF ENGLISH HISTORY only four monarchs have enjoyed a longer reign than Elizabeth II. They are Edward III, Henry III, George III and Queen Victoria. Like her Tudor namesake, Elizabeth came to the throne aged 25 but Elizabeth II celebrated her 70th birthday in 1996, whereas Elizabeth I did not reach hers. Elizabeth II was the eldest daughter of George VI and Lady Elizabeth Bowes-Lyon. She had married Philip Mountbatten in 1947. Her coronation ceremony, in 1953, was a spectacular event.

Above: Queen Elizabeth at her coronation, in 1953. Her reign has become the longest this century and one of the longest in British history.

Below: Elizabeth II's Coronation Crown, now in the Tower of London. It was made in 1660, of gold with over 400 precious and semi-precious stones.

Left: Elizabeth II (1952-) was the eldest daughter of George VI and Lady Elizabeth Bowes-Lyon. She was only 25 when she became queen.

● **1949** Clothes rationing ends. Republic of Ireland is proclaimed. Britain reaffirms position of Northern Ireland in the United Kingdom. Power of the House of Lords is reduced. Apartheid in South Africa begun

● **1950** Scottish Nationalists take Stone of Scone from Westminster (found 1952). General election: Labour majority cut to six. National Service extended to two years (from 18 months). Korean War (to 1953)

● **1951** Festival of Britain. Charges for teeth and spectacles introduced: Labour split. Comet, first jet airliner, developed. General election: Conservatives win majority of 16: Churchill PM

● **1952** George VI dies; succeeded by daughter, Elizabeth II. Identity cards abolished: numbers remain on NH medical cards. Britain makes its first atom bomb. Oil dispute with Iran. Mau Mau disturbances in Kenya. Last London tram runs

● **1953** Queen Elizabeth II's coronation. Disastrous floods on east coast. Myxomatosis reduces rabbit numbers. Commonwealth team climbs Everest. Road transport denationalized. Egypt becomes a republic

● **1954** Tenants gain security of tenure. Hull University founded. "Flying Bedstead" – first vertical takeoff aircraft – developed. Roger Bannister first to run mile in under 4 minutes (3 min 59.4 sec). Food rationing ends. Persian oil dispute settled

● **1955** Winston Churchill retires: Anthony Eden succeeds as PM. General election: Conservatives increase majority to 67. Ruth Ellis is last woman executed for murder. Clement Attlee retires as Labour leader: succeeded by Hugh Gaitskell. Exeter University founded. Duke of Edinburgh's Award Scheme starts. ITV and VHF broadcasts begin

RACE RELATIONS

Until the late 1950s Britain was an almost exclusively white community. But Britain was short of labour after the war and so encouraged immigration from the West Indies, India and Pakistan. Until 1962 anyone from the empire or Commonwealth could come to Britain to live. In 1962 Macmillan's government tried to limit immigration by stating that they must have a job to come to.

The presence of coloured immigrants in large numbers soon resulted in serious racial tensions which the country had not previously experienced. In 1968 many Asians poured in from Kenya and immigration restrictions tightened.

By 1970 the numbers of immigrants had risen to more than one million. To protect these people against racial prejudice in areas such as employment and housing, Parliament passed laws to inflict penalties on people found showing open discrimination, and set up a Race Relations Board to hear complaints and act on them.

Above: **A boatload of immigrants arrives in the 1950s – a time of growth in manufacturing and building after the devastation of war. There was a shortage of labour** and **Britain looked to her ex-colonies, particularly India and the West Indies. Thousands emigrated here, hoping for a good life, but they were paid low wages and met discrimination.**

- **1956** Premium bonds introduced. First Aldermaston march against nuclear weapons. Suez Canal crisis: Anglo-French intervention fails to stop canal's nationalization by Egypt. Suez Canal is blocked

- **1957 Anthony** Eden ill, retires: succeeded by Harold Macmillan as PM. Jodrell Bank radio telescope tracks Sputnik 1 (first satellite). Treaty of Rome signed: Britain does not join EEC. Vietnam War begins (to 1975)

- **1958** Life peerages introduced. Race riots in London and Nottingham. Elizabeth's eldest son, Charles, created Prince of Wales. Last debutantes presented at Court. Fishing dispute with Iceland. British party under Vivian Fuchs makes first trans-antarctic crossing

- **1959** Christopher Cockerell's Hovercraft first Channel crossing. First part of M1 motorway open. General election: Conservatives increase majority to 100. Hawaii becomes 50th US state

Above: **After World War II the United Nations was created to maintain peace and security in the world.**

RHODESIAN INDEPENDENCE

The winding up of the British empire continued rapidly during the 1960s and 1970s. By 1968 all but one of Britain's African colonies had achieved independence. The exception was Rhodesia, formerly Southern Rhodesia, where the white minority held power and was reluctant to give it up. Britain insisted that the black people should be given the right to vote before Rhodesia could be independent. Negotiations between Rhodesia's premier Ian Smith and Britain's Labour prime minister, Harold Wilson, broke down, and on November 11, 1965, Ian Smith declared UDI (unilateral declaration of independence).

Britain ruled that the declaration was illegal, and organized an economic blockade of Rhodesia. Britain was supported by the United Nations. In 1980 the British government was finally able to negotiate a settlement allowing open elections which led to the establishment of a black majority government, at which point what had been Rhodesia was renamed Zimbabwe.

TROUBLE IN NORTHERN IRELAND

Discrimination was a major factor at the root of the troubles in Northern Ireland which broke out in 1969. The partition of Ireland in 1921, which split the six Protestant and Loyalist counties from the rest of the predominantly Catholic south, left a large number of Catholics north of the border. This Catholic minority faced discrimination in terms of housing, job opportunities and influence in local affairs, and began a civil rights movement to press for better conditions.

Civil rights demonstrations were met by counter-demonstrations from the Protestants, who feared any movement which might bring them into association with Eire rather than with Great Britain. Demonstrations quickly turned into mob violence, with deaths and destruction of property on a scale so serious that later in 1969 British troops were sent in to keep order.

Above: **A British soldier patrols a Belfast street. British troops were sent to protect local communities.**

Left: **The 1960s saw the growth of a social, cultural and artistic revolution highlighted by the Beatles, a pop group from Liverpool. Their records sold in millions and their popularity, which was known as Beatlemania, spread all over the world.**

Below: **Pre-decimal coins were based on multiples of twelve instead of the metric multiples of ten we use now.**

DECIMALIZATION

Decimalization involved countries issuing currency in units that are multiples of ten, for example the French franc is made up of 100 centimes. France was the first European country to decimalize its currency during the French Revolution. By the 1870s most other major powers had adopted a decimal system. Britain and its dependencies were the last to change. On February 15, 1971 Britain adopted a decimal system.

- **1960** Seventeen colonies in Africa , and Cyprus, become independent. Pacemaker for hearts developed

- **1961** Volcanic eruption on island of Tristan da Cunha in the South Atlantic: population evacuated to Britain. Farthings cease to be legal tender. Francis Crick and James Watson solve the structure of DNA. South Africa leaves Commonwealth. New universities: Essex and Sussex. Sierra Leone, Tanganyika independent. Yuri Gagarin is first man in space

- **1962** New Coventry cathedral opened. Thalidomide tragedy: babies born with deformities. Independent: Jamaica, Trinidad and Tobago, Uganda. New Act controls immigration from West Indies and Pakistan. London smog: 750 die. First British satellite (Ariel) launched from US space centre at Cape Canaveral

- **1963** Common Market rejects Britain. Beeching Report begins rail closures. Beatles pop group win international fame. Nuclear power station opens at Bradwell. Dartford Tunnel is opened. Peerage Act gives peers right to disclaim on inheritance. Kenya, Malaysia and Zanzibar gain independence. Haorld Macmillan retires: succeeded as PM by Sir Alec Douglas-Home. New universities: Newcastle, York. French president, General Charles de Gaulle, vetoes Britain's entry to the EEC. Britain signs agreement banning nuclear testing

- **1964** Malawi and Zambia independent. New universities: East Anglia, Kent, Lancaster, Strathclyde, Warwick. General election: Labour victory; Harold Wilson becomes PM. Rolling Stones gain popularity

- **1965** Oil, gas found in North Sea. Greater London created. White Rhodesians make unilateral declaration of independence. First woman high court judge appointed

THE ENERGY BOOM

The 1960s and 1970s were an exciting time for British energy and transport development. Oil and natural gas were discovered beneath the North Sea in 1965, which greatly boosted Britain's economic and financial standing in the world. But there was no manufacturing growth or investment in industrial development to take advantage of this new-found wealth.

THE HOVERCRAFT

In 1959, British engineer Christopher Cockerell produced his first hovercraft, the *SRN1* – it crossed from the Isle of Wight to mainland England. In 1965 the first passenger service using hovercrafts started between Britain and France. Hovercrafts ride on a cushion of low-pressure air, blown downwards by fans. The air is held in by a skirt, or side wall, around the hovercraft. This system is ideal for crossing water and landing on beaches or flat land. Hovercraft can easily reach speeds of 120 kilometres an hour They can carry dozens of cars and up to 400 passengers.

JETS AND CARS

Ordinary people were more mobile than ever before. A network of motorways was springing up all over the country – the M1 was opened in 1959, and Spaghetti Junction in Birmingham linked a staggering 18 roads. Cars became sportier and faster, and more and more people could now afford them. Electric and diesel trains took over from steam. People were also now flying for the first time on package holidays to Spain. The first jet airliners, such as the De Havilland *Comet*, came into operation in the early 1960s. In 1969 a *Concorde* prototype made its first flight. *Concorde* became the first supersonic airliner to enter service. It carries up to 144 passengers at twice the speed of sound, and can cross the Atlantic in three hours.

TECHNOLOGICAL CHANGES

Many labour-saving devices that are now taken for granted began to appear in the 1970s – for example, dishwashers, microwave ovens, food mixers and launderettes. Inventor Clive Sinclair introduced the affordable pocket calculator, as well as home computers and digital watches.

Above: **One of many floating offshore oil platforms in the North Sea. The five steel legs of the platform are lowered into the sea in order to anchor it to the seabed. The discovery of oil in the North Sea in the mid-1960s gave Britain the opportunity to transform its economy.**

Below: **Cutaway drawing of the luxury ship *Queen Elizabeth II*, launched in 1967. The liner is 294 metres long and 32 metres wide. It carries a crew of 906 and can accomodate 2,025 passengers.**

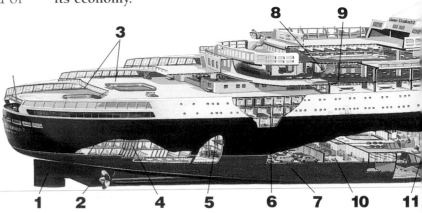

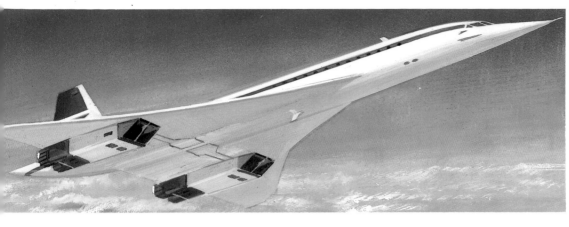

THE COMMON MARKET

The main achievement of Edward Heath's Conservative government was Britain's entry in 1973 into the European Economic Community (EEC), also referred to as the European Community (EC) or the Common Market and more recently as the EU (European Union). Britain declined to join when the EC was formed in 1957, and was turned down when it later changed policy and tried to join in the 1960s. When Labour leader Harold Wilson won the general election of 1974, he negotiated revised terms, and in 1975 invited the public to vote on membership in Britain's first referendum. The vote was a "yes" for staying in the EC. It now comprises 15 Member States: Austria, Belgium, Denmark, Finland, France, Germany, Greece, Ireland, Italy, Luxembourg, The Netherlands, Portugal, Spain, Sweden and the UK. On January 1, 1993, the Single Market came into operation. Its aim is to create a single economic region for people and businesses to travel and trade in freely.

Above: Concorde, the world's only supersonic airliner. Aircraft first broke the sound barrier in the 1940s. Today *Concorde* carries passengers at twice the speed of sound. It was designed and built jointly by Britain and France. The first services were flown in 1976.

Below: **1** Rudder; **2** Screw; **3** Swimming pools; **4** Crew cabins; **5** Car lift; **6** Cabins; **7** Garage; **8** Ballroom; **9** Main lounge; **10** Laundry; **11** Engine room; **12** Stabilizers; **13** Boiler room; **14** Theatre; **15** Reception room; **16** Hospital; **17** Printing shop; **18** Restaurant; **19** Cold stores; **20** Bridge; **21** Bow thrusters; **22** Bow anchor.

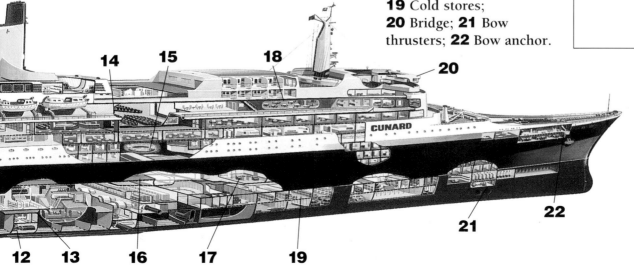

The Maastricht Treaty of 1991 took the Union even further towards a single currency (the ecu, short for European Currency Unit) and a European citizenship that has remained a contentious issue among many members.

THE HEATH AND WILSON YEARS

Economics and labour relations dominated the general elections of the 1970s. In the first, in 1970, most people were confident that the Labour Party would return to power. But in a shock result the Conservatives, under their new leader Edward Heath, won a majority of 31. Britain's heavy international debt was one cause of the defeat.

THE MINERS' STRIKE

In 1974, the miners triggered off the next election. They had been offered a 16 per-cent pay rise but they asked for a pay rise of up to 40 percent, so they threatened to strike. Edward Heath called an election, to get the country's backing for his tough line on wages. The result was a hung Parliament, neither of the two big parties having a majority. Labour took office under Harold Wilson who, after nine months, called a second election which he won with a majority of three.

Left: **Britain and the United States forged a close political alliance under the leadership of Prime Minister Margaret Thatcher (*right*) and President Ronald Reagan.**

MARGARET THATCHER

Margaret Thatcher came to power as Britain's first ever woman prime minister in 1979, having led the Conservatives to election victory over the Labour Party. She became Britain's longest-serving prime minister last century, and the first to win three general elections in a row for over 150 years.

Margaret Thatcher developed what was called the enterprise culture, which was designed to take people away from dependence on the state (and the welfare state). State-owned industries (such as the telephone, gas, electricity and water services) were transferred into the hands of privately-run companies. The nation's health and school services were made more accountable to public spending.

Thatcher was authoritarian with her ministers – all men – and kept a firm control on the reins of power. But her policies are judged to have encouraged material interests and a decline in moral values.

Internationally Thatcher's tough line earned her the nickname the Iron Lady. Her firm direction during the Falklands War, strong opinions, and the special relationship she developed with US president Reagan, won her widespread renown. At home, however, the introduction of the Community Charge, known as the Poll Tax, was extremely unpopular. Designed to replace the local rates system, this – and her increasingly autocratic style – led to her political downfall. Thatcher resigned on November 22, 1990. She was replaced as leader by John Major, who led Britain for the next seven years.

Left: **On 31 March 1990, 200,000 people descended on central London to demonstrate against the unpopular Poll Tax. Thousands of police were deployed to clear violent protesters from Trafalgar Square.**

THE RISE OF NEW LABOUR

The Labour Party floundered during the Thatcher years, racked with internal divisions. Labour leaders Neil Kinnock and John Smith attempted to modernize and broaden the appeal of the party's policies.

However, it took the election of Tony Blair as party leader in 1994 (after John Smith had died of a heart attack) to make Labour a serious political force. Blair immediately set out a new agenda and revamped the Labour Party's platform, with unprecedented commitments to free enterprise, anti-inflationary policies and to greater integration into the European Union. In May 1997, 'New' Labour won a landslide election victory, with a parliamentary majority of 179. The new government soon put into practice various manifesto commitments, including a minimum wage, devolved parliaments for Scotland and Wales, and a complete reform of the House of Lords. Talks about the future of Northern Ireland – which had begun under John Major – were resumed, and a fragile ceasefire was declared in 1998. In 1999, a new Northern Ireland parliament was formed with substantial powers.

Above: **The 135-metre London Eye stands near the River Thames, offering superb views of the capital. It was one of the main attractions in Britain's Millennium celebrations.**

Below: **Prime Minister Tony Blair enjoys a moment with his new son, Leo, born in the year 2000.**

- **1970** Equal pay for men and women decreed by law. General election: Conservatives win with a majority of 31: Edward Heath becomes PM. First use of rubber bullets in Northern Ireland. First *Concorde* landing at Heathrow

- **1971** Open University starts teaching. Decimal currency introduced. Trade union reform introduced. Margaret Thatcher, education minister, abolishes free school milk

- **1972** "Bloody Sunday": 13 killed in Londonderry riots. Northern Ireland comes under direct rule from Whitehall. Asians expelled from Uganda flee to UK. Industrial Relations Court set up. "Bloody Friday" in Belfast: bombs kill 11, wound 120. Miners' strike. Artefacts from Tutankhamun's tomb on display in British Museum: seen by over one million people. Duke of Windsor (formerly Edward VIII) buried at Windsor

- **1973** Britain joins Common Market. IRA car bomb in London kills 1, injures 216, damages Old Bailey. Counties abolished in Northern Ireland. Power cuts lead to three-day week. Bahamas gain independence. Northern Ireland votes to stay in UK. Israel at war with Arabs: Arabs restrict oil, starting world economic crisis

- **1974** Miners vote to strike: Heath calls general election, and loses. Harold Wilson heads minority Labour government. Miners get 35 percent pay rise. English and Welsh counties reorganized. Second general election: Labour majority three

- **1975** Scottish counties abolished. Cod War with Iceland (to 1976). Britain's first referendum: 60 percent vote to stay in EEC

- **1976** Harold Wilson retires: James Callaghan becomes PM. Betty Williams and Mairead Corrigan form Ulster peace movement and win Nobel peace prize (1977)

- **1977** Labour and Liberals form pact. Queen's Silver Jubilee (25 years on throne)

- **1978** First test-tube baby born

- **1979** Winter of discontent: massive series of strikes. Welsh referendum rejects devolution plans; Scots accept by too small a margin. Callaghan loses vote of confidence. General election: Conservatives win overall majority of 43. Margaret Thatcher becomes first woman PM. IRA bomb kills Earl Mountbatten

- **1980** Steel workers strike for 14 weeks. Commandos storm Iranian Embassy to free 19 hostages held there by terrorists. Rhodesia becomes officially independent as Zimbabwe. Callaghan resigns Labour leadership: succeeded by Michael Foot. Jobless top 2,000,000

- **1981** Labour rebels form Social Democratic Party. Ten IRA hunger strikers die

- **1982** Argentina seizes Falkland Islands: re-captured in 10 weeks. Pope visits Britain. Unemployment tops 3,000,000

- **1983** General election: Conservatives have majority of 144. Michael Foot resigns as leader of Labour Party: Neil Kinnock succeeds. IRA car bomb outside Harrods, London kills 6, injures 90

- **1984** Miners begin indefinite strike. Shots from the Libyan People's Bureau in London kill a policewoman. Fire damages York Minster

Left: The Falklands operation would have been impossible without Britain's aircraft carriers. The long flat deck acts as a take-off and landing field. To land, aircraft are guided by radar and radio and by signals from the deck. They are stored below the deck.

THE FALKLANDS WAR

For many years Argentina had claimed the Falkland Islands, which they called the Malvinas, but these had been ruled by Britain since 1833. Argentina's sudden invasion of the islands in the South Atlantic on April 2, 1982, took the world by surprise. Lord Carrington, the foreign secretary, and two of his ministers resigned, feeling that they had seriously misjudged the situation. Theirs was not the only misjudgment: Argentina's rulers did not expect such a swift retaliation by Britain.

With a speed which astonished everyone, Britain sent a task force on its way by sea within three days of the invasion, landing the main force on the Falklands on May 21. In a determined and bloody series of battles, British troops recaptured the Falklands 73 days after the invasion. The United Nations condemned Britain's action, and many felt that the aggressive government response had a political motive with a general election not far away. The Argentines finally surrendered at Port Stanley on June 14. The lives lost were 254 British and 750 Argentinian.

Above: **Some of the 10,000 British troops sent with the task force gathered together in April 1982, to recapture the Falkland Islands from the Argentine invaders. This took 73 days.**

Below: **The British Aerospace Sea Harrier FRS Mk 1 achieved great success in the Falklands conflict of 1982. They destroyed 23 enemy Argentine aircraft without suffering a single loss in air combat.**

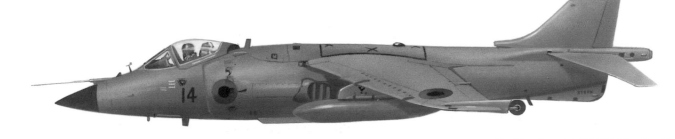

At the end of the war, the problem of the Falkland Islands remained unsolved. Britain refused to negotiate with Argentina on the sovereignty question, insisting that the islanders' wish to remain British be respected. The war also led to a major review of Britain's defence strategy, since several of the warships sent to the Falklands had been on the brink of being scrapped or sold.

Left: **Pope John Paul II, from Poland, the first non-Italian pope since the 16th century. He visited Ireland in 1979 and England in 1982. He took part in a joint service with Robert Runcie, Archbishop of Canterbury, thereby healing a rift between England and Rome that had been opened by Henry VIII in 1534.**

STORMS AND DROUGHTS

It is an old joke that the main subject of conversation in Britain is the weather. But from 1987 onwards weather became a very serious topic. The great hurricane of October 16, 1987 was Britain's worst storm for 250 years. It swept across southern England from Cornwall to East Anglia, killing 18 people, leaving a £300,000,000 trail of damage and felling about 9,000,000 trees. In 1989 Britain had its warmest year since records began in 1659, which brought severe droughts. Then early in 1990 a storm on January 25, killed 45 people. 1995 continued to break records with the hottest summer yet recorded and more droughts which seriously affected people's water supplies.

Above: **Remembering Liverpool football fans who died in the Brussels riots in 1985. Liverpool fans fought a running battle with Juventus supporters from Italy during the European Cup Final at the Heysel Stadium in Brussels. A wall collapsed in the chaos and 38 people were killed. As a result, English teams were banned from European Cup Competitions.**

Left: **Damage caused by the 1987 hurricane.**

- **1984** IRA bomb at Brighton's Grand Hotel, aimed at Conservative leaders during the Party Conference, kills 6 people, injures 31. Britain and China agree over Hong Kong's future. Thames Barrier opened. First Cable TV channels open

- **1985** IRA mortar attack kills 9 policemen in Newry, Ulster. Coal strike ends. Bradford soccer ground blaze kills more than 40 fans. Liverpool fans riot in Belgium: 38 people die. Plane fire at Manchester Airport kills 54. Anglo-Irish agreement is signed. Live Aid concert in London raises £40 million for African famine. High-speed train record – Newcastle to London: 2 hrs 19 mins. Race riots in Brixton, Tottenham, Liverpool

- **1986** Michael Heseltine and Leon Brittan resign from the Cabinet. Channel Tunnel agreement signed. Nuclear reactor explodes, Chernobyl, Soviet Union; fallout reaches Britain. Print-workers strike – violence at Wapping. Queen's visit to China first by British monarch. Halley's Comet

- **1987** Ferry *Herald of Free Enterprise* capsizes: 188 people die. Crazed gunman murders 14 people in Hungerford, Berkshire

THE CHANNEL TUNNEL

Napoleon had once approved plans for a tunnel under the Channel in 1802. In 1880 work was begun and then abandoned by British engineers for fear of an invasion. After more than a century of indecision, Britain and France finally signed an agreement in 1986 to dig the Channel Tunnel to link France and Britain by rail. Work began simultaneously in France and England in 1988. The 56-kilometre-long tunnel was dogged by difficulties. Geological problems caused the project to fall behind schedule, and rising costs led to a financial crisis which was solved early in 1990. Some 15,000 workers helped dig the tunnel, and ten lost their lives. Further problems concerned the rail link from Folkestone to London. The Channel Tunnel finally opened in 1993 and passenger services began in 1994. The journey, taking freight, cars and passengers by electric train, takes 40 minutes.

THE GULF WAR

The forces of Saddam Hussein, the Iraqi leader, overran the neighbouring territory of Kuwait in August 1990, causing the United Nations Security Council to authorize the use of force to remove them if they not withdraw by January 15th. Hussein refused and Allied troops from the United States, Britain, France, Italy, Egypt, Saudi Arabia and other Arab nations went to war on January 17th. Conflict ceased on February 27th, with victory for the Allied forces, in what was called Operation Desert Storm, chiefly due to superior air and fire power. The war witnessed 4,000 bombing missions on the first two days alone. The Iraqis counter-attacked using long-range missiles called Scuds. American Patriot missiles shot many Scuds out of the sky.

The Gulf War caused severe environmental problems because over 600 oil wells had been ignited and oil had been emptied into the sea. Kuwait City had been destroyed and Kuwait ransacked. Over 40,000 people were killed, most of them Iraqi, and Hussein remained an unpredictable force in a still unsettled region.

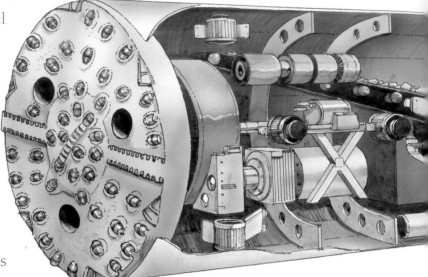

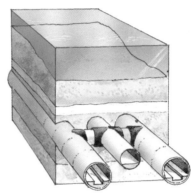

Above: **Cutaway drawing of the Channel Tunnel boring machine.**

Left: **The tunnel is made up of three separate tunnels. Trains run in two of them and the central one is a service shaft.**

Below: **Members of the international coalition who fought in the Gulf War against Iraqi forces.**

In 1991 United Nations troops forced Iraq to withdraw from Kuwait which it had occupied.

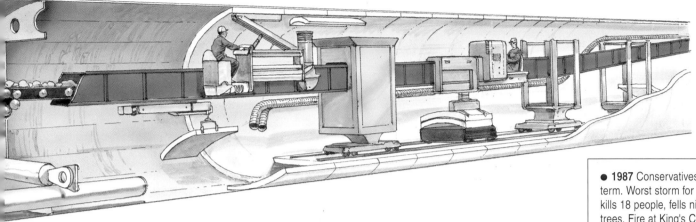

THE HOSTAGE CRISIS

For years Iranian-backed terrorist forces in Beirut had held Western hostages, making a variety of political demands in return for their release. Church of England special envoy Terry Waite made several trips to Beirut to negotiate the release of all the hostages. Waite himself was then captured and held by terrorists for five years.

Long campaigns were conducted by the families and friends of hostages. One of the most notable involved Jill Morrell's poster campaign organized for the release of British journalist John McCarthy. In 1991, after years of negotiations, followed by silence, the hostages were released one by one: journalist John McCarthy on August 8, 1991, after 1,943 days of captivity; September 24, former battle of Britain pilot Jackie Mann kidnapped in May 1989; and on November 18, Terry Waite.

Below: **John McCarthy arrives in England with his father after more than five years in captivity.**

● **1987** Conservatives win third term. Worst storm for 250 years kills 18 people, fells nine million trees. Fire at King's Cross tube station kills 31 people. Terry Waite kidnapped in Beirut. Britain expels 2 Iranian envoys. London stock market collapses. Free dental and eye tests abolished

● **1988** Fire ravages North Sea oil rig *Piper Alpha*: 166 crew die. Triple train crash at Clapham Junction kills 34. Sabotaged airliner crashes on Lockerbie, Dumfriesshire; 270 people die

● **1989** Airliner crashes on MI: 46 die. President Gorbachev of the USSR visits Britain. John Major succeeds Sir Geoffrey Howe as foreign secretary. House of Commons goes on TV. Chancellor of the Exchequer Nigel Lawson resigns; replaced by John Major. Britain's warmest year since 1659. Hillsborough football stadium disaster kills 94. Guildford Four freed

● **1990** A violent storm lashes southern Britain: 45 people die. Hubble Space Telescope launched. Irish hostage Brian Keenan released after four years captivity in Beirut. Iraq invades Kuwait. Parts for Iraqi supergun seized by Customs. Margaret Thatcher resigns as PM: John Major takes over. Strangeways Prison riot and Poll Tax Riot. British and French tunnel workers meet under the Channel. Britain joins the ERM

● **1991** Gulf War (January 17th-February 27th). Allied victory. Hostages John McCarthy and Terry Waite released from Beirut

AUTHOR DENOUNCED

Salman Rushdie's book *The Satanic Verses* roused a worldwide storm amongst Muslims in 1989. Ayatollah Khomeini, then religious leader of Iran, proclaimed that Rushdie was to be sentenced to death by a *fatwah* (order) for his alleged insult to Islam, and called on Muslims to execute him. In Bradford copies of the book were publicly burned. Rushdie was forced into hiding, although he has managed to make several carefully guarded public and television appearances and to publish new novels.

ENVIRONMENTAL ISSUES

Throughout history, humans have had an immense impact on the Earth, as was terrifyingly demonstrated with the first atomic bomb test in 1945. The atomic bomb made people aware, probably for the first time, that future existence on Earth – a planet which is over 4,500 million years old – depended on looking after the environment.

However, despite having a national Department of the Environment in Britain, appalling pollution continues to cause widespread damage. This ranges from litter on the streets, to industrial chemicals in rivers, seas and oceans, car exhaust fumes choking up the atmosphere, and agricultural pesticides destroying plants and animals.

GREEN PRESSURE GROUPS

The environmental pressure group Greenpeace was founded in 1969. Working in 25 countries, Greenpeace has drawn attention to the problems of whaling, seal hunting, sewage pollution and nuclear testing across the world. When it surveyed Britain's coast in 1986, it found disturbing signs of serious pollution from sewage.

Another pressure group called Friends of the Earth was formed in 1971. This group aims to make people (and their governments) aware of vital world issues such as global warming, pollution, the destruction of tropical rainforests and damage to the ozone layer.

The Environmental Protection Agency was formed in England in 1984, and succeeded in helping to ban the trade in elephant ivory. It continues to campaign against the destruction of whales, dolphins and other wildlife; as do

Left: View of the Earth from space. In the 1980s and 1990s fears grew about holes in the ozone layer and global warming.

Below: When there is an oil spill, environmental groups work hard to clean up the coastline and rescue the animals affected. This otter is being cleaned so that it can be safely returned to the wild.

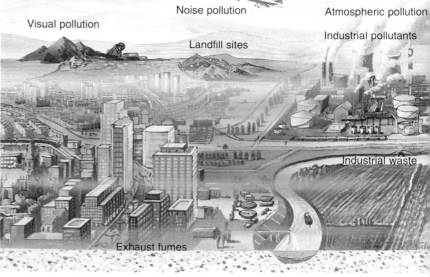

Visual pollution

Noise pollution

Atmospheric pollution

Industrial pollutants

Landfill sites

Industrial waste

Exhaust fumes

the World Wide Fund for Nature UK, the Royal Society for the Protection of Birds, and the Nature Conservancy Council. Biodiversity – the healthy variety and survival of many species – is considered essential to the survival of the planet. All these groups are concerned with protecting the maximum number of animal and plant species and maintaining the highest numbers within each species.

Conservation and green pressure groups have had considerable influence on the government of the day. However, many environmentalists feel that this influence could be greater, and have formed a political party, called the Green Party, to bring pressure on the government from within Parliament. Their message is to treat the Earth like a living thing, and to treat the environment as a living, breathing organism.

Left: **British zoos play a vital role in public education about wildlife and in preservation programmes which aim to increase populations of rare species such as the giant panda.**

RECYCLING

Since the 1970s the idea of recycling different sorts of household rubbish has caught on. In most British towns today there are recycling centres and bottle banks where glass, for example, can be recycled to save all the fuel needed to make new glass, old newspapers and magazines can be recycled to save trees. Most schools have their own projects and various nationally-organized schemes such the BBC Television programme *Blue Peter's* various initiatives have helped everyone to become involved in protecting their environment.

NUCLEAR PROTEST

Britain's testing of nuclear weapons aroused much public alarm. From 1956, protesters made an annual Easter march from the atomic research station at Aldermaston to Trafalgar Square to urge that tests be stopped. In 1958 the Campaign for Nuclear Disarmament (CND) began a campaign to stop the production of British nuclear weapons.

The collapse of communism and the Soviet Union in 1987 meant the end of the Cold War, in which Russia and the United States had threatened each other with nuclear weapons but never used them. Most nuclear powers eventually signed an agreement to ban the testing of nuclear weapons, but in 1995 France provoked world anger by launching a series of nuclear tests in the Pacific Ocean. Again Greenpeace and Friends of the Earth were active in trying to stop these tests.

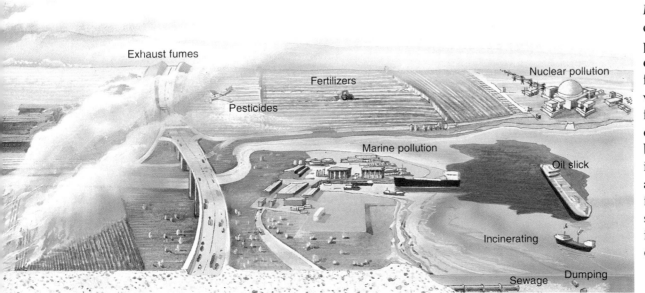

Exhaust fumes

Fertilizers

Pesticides

Nuclear pollution

Marine pollution

Oil slick

Incinerating

Sewage   Dumping

Left: **Some of the causes of pollution: exhaust fumes from road vehicles; smoke from factory chimneys and burning straw; industrial waste, agricultural fertilizers and sewage seeping into rivers and oceans.**

31

FIRE AND DIVORCE

As Queen Elizabeth II herself stated, 1992 was an *"annus horribilis"* – a horrible year for the royal family. Princess Anne divorced, the Duke and Duchess of York separated and Windsor Castle was badly damaged by fire.

A growing number of press and television reports speculated about the future of the marriage of Princess Diana and the future king, Prince Charles. Marital difficulties led to their separation in 1992, which was followed by a divorce in 1996.

DEATH OF A PRINCESS

After the divorce, Diana maintained her high public profile, and worked for and supported many charitable causes, especially children's organizations, AIDS awareness, and landmine casualties in war-torn countries. Her unprecedented popularity in Britain and around the world meant that she was dogged by the press, particularly the paparazzi. It was while trying to escape press attention that Diana, her companion Dodi Fayed, and their driver were killed in a car accident in Paris on 31 August, 1997.

THE FUTURE OF THE MONARCHY

After Diana's death, the Royal Family and their advisors seriously misjudged the mood of the nation, and it was only after pressure from politicians and press that a full state funeral was agreed. Many people saw the Royal Family as cold and uncaring, especially in contrast to the warm and humane image of Princess Diana. Many people began to question why this family should have a special status, and by the end of the 1990s, the future of the British monarchy hung in the balance.

Below: **Princess Diana (1961–1997). In her lifetime, she became far more popular than the Royal Family. In paying tribute to her, Prime Minister Tony Blair described her as the "people's princess".**

Left: **Prince Charles, Prince Harry, Prince William and Diana's brother, Charles (Earl Spencer), watch as Diana's coffin is carried through the streets of London. Princess Diana's death was mourned by people throughout the world, and her funeral watched by many millions on live television.**

- **1992** Conservatives win fourth term. Neil Kinnock resigns as head of Labour Party. Church of England Synod votes to allow women priests

- **1993** Shetlands' oil tanker disaster. IRA bombs in Warrington. Grand National race declared void. Britain ratifies Maastricht Treaty

- **1994** Sunday trading allowed by law. John Smith dies of heart attack: Tony Blair elected as leader of Labour Party. Channel Tunnel passenger services begin. National Lottery introduced

- **1995** John Major fights off challenge for Conservative party leadership. Scott Inquiry into government involvement in the illegal sales of arms to Iraq

- **1996** 16 children and one teacher shot dead at school in Dunblane, Scotland. BSE scare ruins British beef industry. Euro '96: European football championships held in England

- **1997** Labour Party wins General Election with a massive 179 majority. Princess Diana killed in a car crash

- **1998** Peace agreement introduced in Northern Ireland

- **1999** 750 peers lose their hereditary right to sit in the House of Lords. Elections take place for the new devolved parliaments in Scotland and Wales

- **2000** Millennium celebrations in London are a moderate success

- **2001** Foot-and-mouth disease hits Britain. Following attacks on the United States, Britain joins the War Against Terrorism

- **2002** Euro notes and coins go into circulation

RULERS OF BRITAIN

HOUSE	NAME	REIGN	MARRIED	CHILDREN
WINDSOR	George V The House of Saxe-Coburg became the House of Windsor from 1917	1910 – 1936	Victoria Mary of Teck	Edward VIII, George VI, Mary, Henry, George, John
	Edward VIII (Abdicated)	1936		
	George VI	1936 – 1952	Elizabeth Bowes-Lyon	Elizabeth II, Margaret
	Elizabeth II	1952 –	Philip Mountbatten, Duke of Edinburgh (formerly Prince Philip of Greece and Denmark)	Charles, Anne, Andrew, Edward
	The House of Saxe-Coburg became the House of Windsor from 1917			

GLOSSARY

abdication to give up a claim and renounce any right to a duty or office, especially the Crown (as with Edward VIII)

Act a law formally recorded in writing, resulting from a decision taken by Parliament

Allies those powers in World War II including Britain, France, the United States and Russia who opposed Hitler and the Axis powers

appeasement the policy of seeking peaceful solutions to aggressive acts; used to describe Britain's policy to Hitler's expansion before 1939

Axis Germany, Italy and Japan who all wanted more territory and fought the Allies in World War II

cabinet committee of important ministers who, under the prime minister, form the policy of government

colony settlement in a new territory, still subject to its country of origin

Commonwealth voluntary association of independent nations, formerly British colonies

communism a revolutionary brand of Socialism based in theory on workers owning what they produce. In practice it led to the rise of large states where power was in the sole hands of the state leader, such as in Russia and China

conscription a system where citizens are legally bound to serve with the armed forces. In Britain it was introduced from 1916 to 1941

democracy from the Greek *demos*, (the people) and meaning rule by the people. A system of government by elected representatives of the entire adult population of the state

Depression used to refer to an economic slump in the 1930s in Europe (that started in the USA in 1929)

dole term used to describe those unemployed collecting national insurance benefits

dominion colonies of the British Empire that achieved self-governing status

environment the world about us, but usually linked to concerns such as pollution and other global green issues

federation states united under a central government for defence, but independent in internal affairs

IRA Irish Republican Army: terrorist organization seeking to unite Northern Ireland with Eire and using shootings and bombing to achieve that aim

munitions weapons and arms manufactured for a nation's war effort

National Insurance government-backed pensions and other payments to its citizens

Parliament highest body in Britain responsible for making laws, consisting of the House of Commons, the House of Lords and the sovereign

peerage holder of a title such as Duke, Earl, Viscount, passed through a family, allowing that person to sit in the House of Lords. Since 1963 peers can disclaim their titles and sit in the House of Commons

referendum putting issues of national and international importance directly to the people to vote on, rather than making parliament decide on behalf of the public

republic a country governed by a president and parliament-style body, such as France and Ireland. A non-monarchist state

single market referring to the aim of uniting the EU countries into a single economic and monetary and ultimately political union

statute a law or rule made by a body or institution, meant to be permanent and expressed in a formal document; especially, an Act of Parliament

trade unions an association of workers formed to protect their rights and maintain their earnings; started in the 1800s with the Industrial Revolution

INDEX

ACKNOWLEDGEMENTS

The publishers would like to thank the following for supplying additional illustrations for this book:

Picture research: Alex Goldberg, Elaine Willis

page 6, Dublin 1916, Mary Evans Picture Library; p8, Jarrow march, Hulton Deutsch; p15, Digging for Victory, Mark Peppé; p24t, Margaret Thatcher and Ronald Reagan, Corbis; 24bl, Poll Tax demonstrations, Corbis; p25t, London Eye, Corbis; p25br, Tony Blair, Corbis; p29br, John McCarthy, Popperfoto; p32t, Princess Diana, Corbis; 32bl, Princess Diana's coffin, Rex Features